The Beatitudes:

A Profile of The King's Subject

Eli Landrum

Parson's Porch Books
www.parsonsporchbooks.com

The Beatitudes: A Profile of The King's Subject
ISBN: Softcover 978-1-949888-49-2
Copyright © 2018 by Eli Landrum

All rights reserved. No part of this book may be reproduced or transmitted in any form or by any means, electronic or mechanical, including photocopying, recording, or by any information storage and retrieval system, without permission in writing from the publisher.

The Beatitudes:
A Profile of The King's Subject

To my family, with love and with appreciation for all you have contributed to my life

Contents

Introduction 9

Poor in Spirit 17
    Matthew 5:3

Grief-Stricken 24
    Matthew 5:4

Disciplined 33
    Matthew 5:5

Insatiable Appetite for Righteousness 41
    Matthew 5:6

Merciful 50
    Matthew 5:7

Pure in Heart 59
    Matthew 5:8

Peacemakers 69
    Matthew 5:9

Persecuted 76
    Matthew 5:10

Believing Without Seeing 84
    John 20:29

Receiving Consummate Congratulations 87
    Revelation 14:13

Conclusion 90

Selected Bibliography 93

Introduction

> *"After John was put in prison, Jesus went into Galilee, proclaiming the good news of God. 'The time has come,' he said. 'The kingdom of God is near. Repent and believe the good news!'"* (Mark 1:14-15, NIV).

Mark, probably the first Gospel writer, highlighted the beginning of Jesus' public ministry by capsuling His ringing message. The brief summary warrants close examination in order for us to understand the import and urgency of Jesus' proclamation.

Jesus had journeyed from His hometown of Nazareth in Galilee, the northern section of the promised land, to Judea, the southernmost area of the land. He went to undergo John's baptism to signify His approval of John's ministry, to take His stand with others who were responding positively to John's message, and to signify the beginning of His public ministry. He had no sin of which to repent, but He openly identified with the movement that began with John's appearance on the scene and to indicate He was the One whose way John was preparing.

Following Jesus' baptism, the Spirit sent Jesus into the desert region where He stayed for forty days (a lengthy period corresponding with the Israelites' forty-years' wandering in the wilderness). That is, He was sent away to be by Himself. During that time, Jesus coped with temptations. Matthew spelled out the temptations, clearly revealing they had to do with what kind of Messiah Jesus would be. Jesus emerged from the forty days of inner struggle determined to be the Suffering Servant Messiah of Isaiah 52:13—53:12 who would suffer and die vicariously for people's sins, thus opening a way of grace to relationship with God. The Israelites had given in to temptation and had failed to be God's missionary people; Jesus was victorious over temptation and would fulfill God's redemptive purpose.

Because John the Baptist had dared to condemn Herod Antipas's taking his brother Phillip's wife and marrying her, which John labeled unlawful, Herod had imprisoned John and later acquiesced to a request for his death. Jesus saw John's imprisonment as a signal to begin His public ministry. Evidently Jesus had returned to Nazareth. When He heard John was incarcerated, He traveled throughout the region of Galilee, in which Nazareth was located, preaching the message that was the focal point of His ministry.

Jesus would become renowned as a superbly effective, insightful, and authoritative teacher. Yet He began His public ministry by "proclaiming the good news of God" (Mark 1:14). The Greek word translated "proclaiming" has the sense of continuous action and means "to announce openly" as a herald, "to preach." The term always carries "a suggestion of formality, gravity, and an authority which must be listened to and obeyed." Jesus' message was direct, urgent, and called for response. Somewhere I ran across the statement that preachers are of three kinds: those to whom people cannot listen, those to whom people will listen, and those to whom people must listen. Jesus was solidly in the last category.

Jesus preached "the good news of God." The word gospel gathers up the idea of Jesus' phrase. The Greek term behind the words "good news" first meant "a reward for good tidings" and then the good tidings itself. The phrase "of God" is packed with crucial meaning. First, it designates God as the source of the good news being published. The news was good because of its gracious Originator. Second, the content of the news was what God was doing through Jesus of Nazareth. God was offering grace and mercy to sinners totally incapable of extricating themselves from sin's deadly grip. He was offering relationship with Him as a gift motivated solely by His incredible, underserved love for all people.

Jesus' announcement that "the time [had] come" (v. 15) emphasized the significance of His message and ministry. The time to which He referred was not primarily chronological time but was a season of opportunity that God determined—a fitting, suitable period of time, a signal juncture in history. In God's perfect timing, He took on human form and both became and announced the good news of available grace for people's lostness. Jesus' appearance on the scene marked the crucial point in human history.

Jesus heralded that "the kingdom of God [was] near." God's kingdom is not a realm and is not to be identified as the church or the world. God's kingdom is His sovereign rule. In a real sense, God is Sovereign Ruler of His universe (of everything, of all that is) whether or not people recognize and accept His rule. Yet for people who through faith in Christ place themselves under His rule, God becomes the beneficent Sovereign, the Heavenly Father whose power and authority are exercised with compassion. People must decide to remain rebels against the sovereign King or to become His subjects. Their ultimate destiny hinges on that crucial choice.

The phrase "is near" literally is "has drawn near," "has approached" [Greek text]. The idea is that in Jesus, God's kingdom was pressing in on or confronting people. In Jesus, God's kingdom had drawn so near as to be breaking into human history, Thus, people were forced to make life-determining decisions concerning Jesus' identity. They had to choose to be God's willing, committed subjects or to reject His offer of grace.

Jesus appealed to people who heard His message to "repent and believe the good news." The term "repent" has the idea of changing one's mind and thus of changing life's direction—of doing an about-face. It has the sense of turning away from sin, self-will, self-absorption and turning toward God. It includes sorrow for sin but basically involves living in a new direction. Believing the good news of available grace and mercy included accepting it as truth or fact but involved much more. The Greek word for "believe" means "to place confidence in" but also has the force of obedience and commitment. To believe the gospel meant—and means—to make a faith-commitment to the Christ of the gospel.

Jesus called four fishermen as His first disciples and then embarked on an extensive tour of Galilee, engaging in a ministry of teaching, preaching, and healing. At some point, He looked out over the throng of people following Him, went up a mountainside, and sat down (a teacher's usual custom). His disciples drew near, and in the background the crowd waited expectantly. The words "He began to teach them" introduce what has come to be known as the Sermon on the Mount. The phrase could be translated "He was teaching them" or "He customarily taught them," possibly pointing to chapters 5—7 as a compilation of Jesus' teachings.

I have no doubt that Matthew 5—7 was designed to meet a crucial need in the early church's life. The extensive teachings offered clear and challenging guidelines for Christian living. These were Jesus' words to His followers. They heard the words, not as spoken in the past, but as being spoken in the present by their risen Lord, thus authoritative and expecting obedience.

Significantly, Matthew 5:3-12 begins the Sermon by describing what a follower of Jesus looks like. Jesus summoned people to become subjects in God's kingdom and then characterized those subjects. One definition of the word subject is a person "under the authority or control of, or owing allegiance to, another." To become God's subjects through faith in Christ was—and is—the beginning of a spiritual journey, not a culmination. It was—and is—the start of a process of spiritual growth that extends through a lifetime.

Jesus gave a distinct and challenging profile of a kingdom citizen. As I write, the words profile and profiling often are used in a negative sense as assuming the worst or likely guilt of a class of people. For example, some people use the phrase "racial profiling" to indicate a tendency to assume that a particular race of people are prone to criminal behavior and thus are prime targets for law enforcement. The term profile, however, also has positive meanings.

One dictionary defines the term profile as "an outline," "a short, vivid biography." A second definition is "a short description of someone or something that gives important and useful details about them (sic)." A profile can be a drawing or a side view of someone's face. When our first grandson was quite young, our daughter and son-in-law gifted us with an artist's remarkable profile—a side view—of his face. In every detail, it was unmistakably his handsome little face. With well-chosen, powerful, and highly suggestive words Jesus presented a profile of a person under

God's rule, a kingdom subject. "We should think not so much of eight different types of character as of one ideal character seen from eight different angles—one diamond with eight facets." Under God's sovereign rule, a person becomes uniquely different in character and conduct or lifestyle. Jesus' profile is known as the Beatitudes (blessed sayings). The title comes from the first word in each of Jesus' brief declarations. We will look closely at the Greek term when we explore the first saying.

Poor in Spirit

Matthew 5:3

"Blessed are the poor in spirit, for theirs is the kingdom of heaven."

We can describe people in terms of physical appearance: height, weight, hair and eye color, facial features, and distinctive mannerisms. When we know others well, we can refer to intangibles: They are congenial, loving, caring, kind, generous, and humorous. What are the character traits of a kingdom citizen? Put another way, what does a committed, loyal Christian look like as he or she engages in the give-an-take of daily life? Jesus began His lengthy discourse (or Matthew began his compilation of Jesus' teachings) with an easily memorized description of people who placed themselves under God's rule.

In the first of three great reversals or contrasts, Jesus pronounced "the poor in spirit" to be "blessed." The Greek term translated "blessed" can mean "happy" or "fortunate." Behind the word, however, lies a progression from a secular use applied to externals to an elevated spiritual meaning. Originally, the term may have meant "great" and may have been limited to material prosperity with the sense of wealth or riches. Among philosophers the word took on a moral sense: happiness derived from moral correctness and knowledge. In the Scriptures, the term is elevated to the level of the spiritual. "In the Old Testament, the idea involves more of outward prosperity than in the New Testament, yet it almost universally occurs in connections which emphasize, as its principle element, a sense of God's approval founded in righteousness which rests ultimately on love to God....It becomes the express symbol of a happiness identified with pure character." William Barclay wrote that "the Beatitudes are not promises of future happiness; they are congratulations on present bliss," what he termed divine bliss.

To me, "happy" seems to be a rather weak and misleading translation of the word Jesus used. Our English word happy goes back to the root hap that means "chance" or "good luck." The emotion we label "happy" depends on favorable circumstances. Landing a dream job, receiving a promotion or a raise in pay, and enjoying a well-funded retirement bring a sense of elation and satisfaction. At my stage in life, a good doctor's report lifts my spirits greatly. I don't think Jesus had that kind of pleasant feeling in mind. I think He meant the poor in spirit were to be congratulated because they had God's approval. They were on the right track in life and had God's commendation. They received God's positive estimation of their condition in all the chances and changes of life.

That we understand clearly the phrase "the poor in spirit" is crucial. Luke wrote, "Blessed are you who are poor" (Luke 6:20). Some interpreters have suggested that Matthew correctly clarified Jesus' intended meaning. In this view, Luke reflected the Old Testament's emphasis on the pious poor "who out of their need cast themselves wholly on God for their salvation." The Greek language has two words that mean "poor." One term was used for people who depended on daily wages to survive. They literally eked out a living—they lived "from hand to mouth." The second word expressed abject poverty, utter destitution. It was used of someone reduced to begging to survive. The word "is connected with [a root term] which means to cower or to crouch; and it describes the poverty which is beaten to its knees." Jesus used the second term to describe people who realized they were spiritually bankrupt, spiritually impoverished, and who turned to God for forgiveness and relationship with Him. They realized and acknowledged that He alone could provide the grace and mercy they so desperately needed. We need to be clear that the phrase "poor in spirit" does not describe a person whose life experiences have broken his or her spirit or have beaten the individual down into despair. Certainly, many people live in that place. Neither do the words describe a person who is mean-spirited, lacking spirit (vitality), or weak in faith. Jesus described an individual who had a clear-eyed view of being spiritually impoverished and of the need to plead God's mercy. Clarence Jordan pointed out that the opposite of poverty of spirit is pride, and pride keeps a person out of the kingdom.

Material poverty was a tragic reality in Jesus' day and remains so in our time. Being poor is not a blessing. Being destitute of life's basic necessities does not produce the emotion of happiness. One aim of the Christian gospel is to eliminate abject poverty. Governments wrestle with implementing ways to eliminate the plight of people who are poverty-stricken. The Christian view of life does not advocate voluntary poverty as a mark of genuine religion; it does advocate a correct attitude toward money and the correct use of it to help the destitute. Being poor brings no blessing. In addition, the poor can be as money-centered, greedy, and selfish—as wrongly motivated—as the wealthy. Poverty can produce a hard and bitter attitude. The poor can be proud in spirit, even as the rich can be poor in spirit.

Something is terribly wrong when such a much-too-large percentage of people in the world's richest country—our nation—goes to bed every night hungry. We cannot use Jesus' statement in John 12:8, "You will always have the poor among you," as a rationalization for not working to alleviate poverty. Two mission trips involving people in my church keep me in touch with pockets of abject poverty and keep me uneasy with my meager contributions. One yearly mission is to an impoverished area in Tennessee; the other is to the island nation of Haiti. Gut-wrenching pictures of people with little or nothing drive home the seriousness of Jesus words in Matthew 25:31-46 about seeing Him in the world's needy people and either moving to help them or ignoring their plight. People who are the objects of His love and concern demand our compassionate actions. The poor are always with us, and they must remain as worthy of our efforts to address their plight.

Translations and paraphrases have attempted to capture the force of Jesus' words in Matthew 5:3. The Holy Bible: Contemporary English Version reads: "God blesses those people who depend only on him." J. B. Phillips translated: "How happy are the humble-minded." Charles B. Williams rendered the first phrase, "Blessed are those who feel poor in spiritual things." William Barclay well may have captured the force of Jesus' words best: "Blessed is the man who has realized his own utter helplessness, and who has put his whole trust in God." The poor in spirit are people who clearly recognize their inability to provide their salvation through their own efforts; they cannot earn forgiveness and relationship with God. They realize they can only throw themselves on God's mercy and ask to receive His grace. Clarence Jordan saw the key element in Jesus' declaration to be the clear recognition of need as "the first essential to kingdom citizenship."

In one of His parables, Jesus provided commentary on the contrast between spiritual self-confidence or arrogance and casting oneself on God's mercy and grace. Two men—a Pharisee and a tax collector—went to the temple to pray. The Pharisee practically congratulated God for having such a fine fellow as he was among His people. He thanked God that he was better than sinful people—and better than the tax collector within his scope of vision. The tax collector stood off to one side, his face downcast. He struck his chest as an expression of his guilt. He cast himself on God's mercy, calling himself "the sinner"— perhaps viewing himself as foremost among sinners. Jesus shocked His audience by declaring that the tax collector, not the Pharisee, left the temple having been made right with God and set on the right path in life. The tax collector recognized his spiritual poverty and threw himself on God's mercy, receiving grace for his need (Luke 18:9-14).

The words "theirs is the kingdom of heaven" express the truth that people who recognize their spiritual poverty and cast themselves on God's mercy are welcomed as His subjects. The phrase "the kingdom of heaven" reflects the Jews' aversion to using the name "God," holding it to be so sacred that terms were to be substituted for it. Thus, Matthew's phrase is a synonym for "the kingdom of God." People who turned to God out of a spiritual need they could not supply came under His gracious rule. Eugene Peterson paraphrased the first beatitude: "You're blessed when you're at the end of your rope. With less of you there is more of God and his rule."

One of my New Testament professors in seminary pointed out that being subjects in God's kingdom— being under His beneficent rule—is not the promise of reward but a statement of fact. Alfred Plummer wrote:

"This is not the reward of…being poor in spirit, but the result of it. It is not so much a question of recompense but of consequence."

A subject of the King is first of all a person who in utter dependence on God pleads His mercy and grace to do what the individual cannot do: extricate himself/herself from sin's deadly grasp. That person begins new life under God's gracious rule.

Grief-Stricken

Matthew 5:4

"Blessed are those who mourn, for they will be comforted."

After a long, courageous battle against cancer, my neighbor and friend died at the relatively young age of 60. His wife asked that I take part in his memorial service, giving my reflections on my relationship with him. I did so. After the attendees moved to the interment site, I read a brief Scripture passage and remained standing as the interment proceeded. From where I stood, I had a direct, clear view of my friend's wife and two sons, and their sharp-edged grief moved me deeply. I shared their grief as far as I could. That experience continues to remind me that if a universal emotion exists, it is grief over loss—loss of parents, spouses, children, relationships, jobs, dreams, self-respect. Sooner or later, each of us has been or will be grief-stricken.

The Beatitudes (blessed sayings) give us a comprehensive profile of the complex and exemplary character of the King's subject. Each facet of the kingdom citizen's make-up is held up to us so that we may see the qualities God's person has and displays. Jesus was definite as He spoke. If we are His followers and are under God's rule, we are—or are on the way to becoming—the people He described. Kingdom subjects are of a unique and extraordinary kind.

In the first Beatitude, the first of three great reversals or contrasts, Jesus congratulated the "poor in spirit." People who recognize and acknowledge their utter spiritual destitution—their spiritual bankruptcy—receive God's approval, for they are prepared to throw themselves on His mercy and grace, the decisive commitment by which people enter God's kingdom—come under His beneficent rule.

In Jesus' second great contrast between human and divine assessment or evaluation, He made another startling statement: "Blessed are those who mourn, for they will be comforted." What a paradox: The mourners receive God's congratulations! Jesus' use of the universal experience of sorrow no doubt riveted His hearers' attention.

The term translated "mourn" Jesus used is the strongest word for sorrow in the Greek language. It was used for grieving for people who had died, expressing strong lament for a loved one. In the Septuagint (a major Greek translation of the Hebrew Scriptures), it was used of Jacob's deep grief when he thought his son Joseph was dead. (See Genesis 37:34-35.) The word conveys the idea of grief that cannot be hidden; it must be expressed. "It is a sorrow which is poignant, piercing and intense." Clarence Jordan pointed out that "a mourner is not necessarily one who weeps. He is one who expresses deep concern. Tears are not essential to mourning, but deep concern is." He added that "mourners are really those who are concerned to the point of action." Tears can be a genuine expression of sorrow, but they are not the only response.

How can heart-wrenching sorrow be an occasion for congratulations? Most of us know from experience or have observed that grief cannot be labeled "good," and it is not something to be welcomed. Sometimes, sorrow is too deep to be expressed verbally; other times, grief can only be expressed through weeping. No one who has seen genuine sorrow etched into a human face can say grief is a blessing or can connect it with the emotion of happiness. Instead, it contorts faces and banishes joy.

In Jesus' statement, "Blessed are those who mourn," He did not mean that all people who grieve are to be congratulated, even as he did not mean that all who are poor are to be congratulated. Charles Allen, an insightful Methodist pastor of an earlier generation, wrote: "[Jesus was] not talking about the pessimist who constantly looks for the bad, nor of the selfish person whose ambitions have been thwarted, nor of the person who is bitter and rebellious over some loss." That is, Jesus did not have in mind the person who constantly expects the worst or the individual who bemoans impending bad luck, actual or imagined, or the person who complains because everything has not worked out like he or she planned. In actuality, some sorrow is well-earned: grief that comes when selfishness is frustrated. Jesus was not indicating that Christians' wearing a sad face has any merit. Let's face it: being a Christian does not mean we feel the emotion of happiness all the time, for following Jesus involves sharing His sorrow. Yet even that grief is not to be equated with true piety.

I think Jesus' reference to "those who mourn" includes grief His followers experience in the course of living. Christians suffer loss like everybody else. They experience tragedies, difficulties, and hurts in life's give-and-take. Loved ones die; relationships end abruptly; jobs are terminated; health begins to decline. In these and other instances, God comforts His people.

My church has a rack of cards that members can take and send to people to express care. One card expresses sympathy and features a quote of Matthew 5:4, assuring those who grieve that they will receive comfort. This well may be one emphasis of Jesus' words. I am convinced, however, that this was not Jesus' primary reference.

Jesus basically had in mind grief that has its inception in an acute sensitivity to wrong, suffering, and need. One of the most tragic experiences of any person is loss, and nothing is more tragic than the loss of one's moral and spiritual sensitivity. In Ephesians 4:19, Paul wrote about people who had "lost all sensitivity."

When we no longer react to evil conditions in and around us, we have entered an extremely dangerous state. What the world in general considers to be a weakness is actually one of the most desirable traits of character: the ability to feel, and to feel deeply. The capacity to grieve is the opposite extreme of the capacity to experience joy; the capacity to suffer spiritually is linked inseparably to the ability to exercise spiritual discernment. When one can feel, it is a matter of congratulations, not regret. The real regret comes when we can no longer feel. The calloused person is to be pitied because that individual's cynicism and callousness robs the person of the joy of feeling pleasure to the highest level. Christianity is caring. The ability to care opens up the distinct possibility of sorrow and suffering.

The king's subject mourns because the individual realizes his or her spiritual bankruptcy; sorrow arises out of the seriousness of personal sin This is the person described in Psalm 51:17 as having "a broken spirit; a broken and contrite heart." David, most likely the psalm's writer, was a prime example, expressing his remorse after the prophet Nathan confronted him with his sins surrounding his ruthless actions in taking Bathsheba for himself.

A citizen of God's kingdom feels keenly the King's attitude toward wrong. George Buttrick wrote: "Others [outside the kingdom] are content with an unexamined life; sin to them is a trivial affair." Personal wrong, however, is no trivial matter to the King's subject. In Romans 7:15-19, Paul expressed his deep personal pain concerning his tendency toward sin. This agonizing grief is a necessity for genuine repentance, for a person who truly sorrows because of personal sin will be moved to do something about it. William Barclay wrote: "The way to the joy of forgiveness is through the desperate sorrow of the broken heart." Before we can deeply want forgiveness and have the attitude of repentance, through which it can be given, we must know that our wrong is close kin to the kind of wrong that fashioned a cross and created a Calvary—the kind of sin that could "take the loveliest life in all the world and smash it on a Cross.' "The second [Beatitude] tells us we should be so grieved over our moral and spiritual shortcomings that we cannot rest until we have found God."

Often, I hear and read a rather flippant rationalization for blatant wrongdoing: "After all, I am only human." That kind of casual dismissal of personal sin reveals a dismal failure to recognize that true confession and repentance require a clear recognition of sin's seriousness. It also shows a woefully inadequate view of forgiveness. It is an excuse devoid of the recognition that sin is the result of a deliberate choice for which one is accountable. Accepting that accountability by confessing, having genuine sorrow for the sin, and truly repenting brings forgiveness. Each element must be involved.

The kingdom citizen mourns for personal sin. In addition, the person grieves over the wrong he or she observes being committed by others. Morally and spiritually sensitive, the individual reacts to the evil in the world at large. The kingdom subject experiences sorrow for a world torn by strife. People cannot get along with one another, and peace continues to be elusive. The Christian grieves over a world in which many people have gone berserk in their drive for wealth, power, and control over others. Often, in my prayers, I ask that God move the human race to sanity and a deep sense of humaneness. "Man's inhumanity to man"—what one writer of fiction terms "moral insanity"—continues in word-wide scope and intensity.

I walk on my treadmill for exercise. In the room is a television set I watch that allows me to largely ignore the aches and pains of age as I walk. Late one afternoon, I watched a news report on the civil war in Syria. The report focused on doctors who volunteered to enter war zones to extend medical care to innocent, helpless victims of the conflict. Because hospitals—some of them with maternity wards and neonatal units—were deliberately bombed, makeshift medical facilities were set up in caves. I reacted with shock, anger, and grief at a fresh realization of the depths of evil to which some humans can sink. My experience has increased the intensity of my praying for a rise to moral sanity.

The King's subject grieves over evil's entrenchment in some human hearts. The subject also sorrows when he or she views a world largely disinterested in committed, exacting discipleship to Christ. The person mourns because of the indifference of too many Christians to the matter of their participation in telling the good news of Christ, as though this is an elective they can choose or refuse. For the kingdom subject, the plight of non-Christians is not a source of glee or comfort. Rather, he or she experiences genuine sorrow because of their unbelief.

Jesus may have intended an additional facet of the kingdom subject's grief: a voluntary sharing of others' pain. One who does so has God's approval or congratulations, for that individual has the capacity to feel to some degree others' suffering. Granted, doing so is not easy. Often, the King's subject is dealing with his or her own pain. So, he or she could sidestep becoming involved with others' problems. Yet the Christian opens himself/herself up to others' misery, suffering, and pain. These are the believers Jesus described in Matthew 25:34-36 as feeding the hungry, providing drink for the thirsty, extending hospitality, clothing the destitute, tending the sick, and visiting prisoners. They are compassionate, and their reward is to grow in compassion.

Sorrow generated by others' pain is not the attitude or stance of standing at a distance, removed from people and conditions and feeling bad about their wrong or suffering. The sorrow of the King's subject moves that person to attempt corrective action. The second Beatitude shows us that being detached from people is never right. Attachment to people can result in our getting hurt, but it also moves us to redemptive action.

Jesus said that believers who sorrow receive God's congratulations, for they will be comforted. The term

He used for "comforted" has the sense of being encouraged or animated. The idea is that God comes alongside His subject, not at some future time but as the person sorrows over sin and suffering. He gives supporting strength and the bracing assurance that the person is forgiven and is on the right track, headed in the right direction. J. B. Phillips's paraphrase catches the emphasis of Jesus' words assuring believers "who know what sorrow means" that "they will be given courage and comfort."

Disciplined

Matthew 5:5

"Blessed are the meek, for they will inherit the earth."

From time-to-time, people have posted on Facebook stunning pictures of magnificent horses. The animals have sleek coats with beautiful coloration. Their most awesome feature is their huge size. They are gigantic and extremely muscular, and the overall impression I get is awesome power barely contained. What are the odds that anyone would describe them with the word meek? I seriously doubt anyone would. Yet as we will see, understood in the sense Jesus used the term, it would be an appropriate description.

At first reading, the third great reversal or contrast Jesus stated at the beginning of the Sermon on the Mount is perhaps the most puzzling and shocking. He declared that the "meek" are to be congratulated, "for they will inherit the earth." His words are especially surprising because we do not normally think of meek people as meriting congratulations, and we certainly do not think of them as possessing or taking over the earth. Conversely, our society in general congratulates and awards the aggressive, self-assertive, hard-charging individuals who force their way to the top. So much so that I recall seeing an advertisement years ago that touted a how-to book on a person's becoming more aggressive and assertive in order to be successful. The generally accepted view seems to be that forceful, assertive people win; they accumulate wealth, wield power, and gain others' admiration. Yet Jesus said that the meek receive the highest possible accolade: God's congratulations.

Meekness is the third facet of the character of the King's subject. Jesus described Himself as "gentle (meek) and humble in heart" (Matthew 11:29). In describing "the fruit of the Spirit," Paul included "gentleness (meekness)" (Galatians 5:22-23). The Holy Bible: New International Version translated the Greek word Jesus and Paul used in terms of gentleness, perhaps to avoid a surface misunderstanding. Paul made an important point: Only the Holy Spirit (God's presence) within a believer can produce the character quality of meekness. This facet is not self-generated. Jesus emphasized that the King's subject will have and demonstrate this quality.

What do you normally think of when you hear a person described as meek? My guess is that the general tendency is to equate "meek" with "weak." The dictionary definition of the term meek largely reinforces this tendency. The word meek is defined as "patient and mild; not inclined to anger or resentment....tamely submissive....too submissive;

spiritless." Suggested synonyms are "humble" and "modest."

The Greek word for "meek" Jesus used has a wealth of meaning that is not resident in our use of the term. The Greek word means "gentle," "kind," "forgiving," "benevolent," and" humane." A form of the term means "forbearance." In classical Greek, applied to people, it meant "gracious." Most significantly, the term was used of strong animals who had been domesticated, such as horses that were taught to respond to reins. Meekness has about it the quality of being teachable, of being open to instruction. It is a willingness to learn and to be corrected. It not only involves being self-disciplined but also of accepting discipline. Meekness includes the continuing cultivation and application of discipline. It is self-discipline in the sense that we first have accepted God's discipline and control. We have placed ourselves under His sovereign rule.

I have found that one of my greatest needs at this point in my life is self-discipline, self-control. I also have found that it cannot be self-generated. I try to start out each day with a brief prayer, one petition of which is that God will help me have self-discipline for that day. Usually, the day is still young when I mess up and have to begin again.

The "meek" are believers "who suffer wrong without bitterness or desire for revenge, a class who in this world are apt to go to the wall." Meekness has been defined, not as total submission to all injustice and wrong, but as "the opposite of sudden anger, of malice, of long harboured (sic) vengeance." The meek are not Christians without backbone or courage. George Buttrick described the meek as believers who "are not harsh, not self-assertive, not covetous, not trampling in brute force....Others claim their rights, but the meek are concerned about their duties....The meek walk in quiet godliness"

Before the New Testament period, the term meek was never used in a negative sense, but Jesus and subsequent New Testament writers took the word and raised it to an even higher level to express a higher good. In pre-Christian usage, the term was used to mean "mild" or "gentle." "It was applied to inanimate things, as light, wind, sound, and sickness. It was used of a horse; gentle....Aristotle defines it as the mean between stubborn anger and that negativeness of character which is incapable of even righteous indignation....Plato opposes it to fierceness or cruelty, and uses it of humanity to the condemned....Pinder applies it to a king, mild or kind to the citizens, and Heroditus uses it as opposed to anger."

In the pre-Christian uses, the term meek described outward conduct as related to others. Moses was described as being "a very humble (meek) man, more humble (sic; meeker) than anyone else on the earth" (Numbers 12:3). The Hebrew word can be translated "humble," "lowly," or "meek." This certainly does not mean Moses was weak, mild, or timid. In contrast, he was strong and forceful when he needed to be. The Christian use of the word refers to an inward quality in a person's relationship with God. It expresses all it meant to pagans—gentleness, kindness, patience—but it goes well beyond that. These expressions toward people are the demonstrations of the new life in Christ.

Christian meekness does not mean mildness that comes from lack of courage. Rather, it describes a gentleness of strength that knows how and when to be mild or to be forceful. The Jesus who described Himself as gentle (meek) was the same Jesus who drove the money-changers and traders from the court of the Gentiles in the Jerusalem temple. This strong, forceful Jesus also could take children in His arms and bless them in the presence of the people who brought them (see Mark 10:13-16). William Barclay wrote that "there is gentleness in [meekness] but behind the gentleness there is the strength of steel....[Meekness] is not a spineless gentleness, a sentimental fondness, a passive quietism. It is a strength under control."

Archibald Thomas Robertson, a New Testament scholar of a previous generation, defined meekness in terms that resonate with me. He defined the Greek word as a blend of "spiritual poise" and strength—the ability to remain calm, composed, and strong no matter what the circumstances may be. A beagle who is one of my favorite cartoon characters, stated—as a beagle scout leader—that two responses to crises exist: to panic or to remain calm and collected. He chose to panic. A common phrase in use today as a synonym for poise is "keeping your cool." The phrase and idea are light years from being original. It was in vogue during my teen years. In researching commentary material on the third beatitude, I read Matthew Henry's reflections. He wrote in the 18th century and stated: The meek are those "who can be cool while others are hot."

In the New Testament, meekness is the priceless ability to keep one's head in situations that could cause a person to go to pieces. In daily give-and-take, poise is the quality that is necessary for success. The sports team that finds itself in extreme difficulty has a chance for victory if it keeps its poise. The person in the workaday world advances when the individual displays calmness and clear thinking in tense situations. The individual to whom others look in times of trouble is one who retains poise. Jesus stressed that spiritual poise (composure) is necessary in a world in which people who live His kind of life will meet opposition and difficulty. Spiritual poise is not indifference or aloofness to situations and other people. It is composure that issues from a relationship with the King.

Jesus demonstrated spiritual poise consistently throughout His life, even in His death. Granted, He once described Himself as meek and lowly, but the words cannot be taken to mean He was timid, shy, or weak. Far from being weak, He was supremely poised with disciplined strength, an inner quality we are to have the King's subjects.

Jesus said that the meek "will inherit the earth." The Greek word translated "inherit" basically means "obtain," "acquire," "receive possession of." If the approach is correct that this is not a promise to be fulfilled in the future but a present reality, it cannot mean that one day believers will own all the world's real estate, that they will acquire the entire globe. What, then, can Jesus' statement mean?

This third beatitude is a direct quote of Psalm 37:11: "The meek will inherit the land." The entire psalm is an assurance to God's people that if they trusted in the Lord and did good, they would live in peace in the land He had given them. In verse 9, the psalmist declared that those who hoped in God would "inherit the land." In verse 22, he affirmed that those whom the Lord blessed would "inherit the land." In verse 29 the writer stated that the righteous would "inherit the land and dwell in it forever." In verse 34 he counseled his people to "wait for the Lord and keep his way"; as a result, God would "exalt [them] to inherit the land."

By quoting part of Psalm 37:11, Jesus likely had in mind the entire psalm—the assurance that God's purpose will come to fulfillment. His people are to trust Him, live as He directs, and wait expectantly for Him to act. They are not to lose heart at evil's seeming triumph. Because they participate in His redemptive purpose, even now they share in His triumph. In the statement "they will inherit the earth," Jesus meant that at the present moment God's people are taking part in God's victorious cause. Disciplined, poised, teachable Christians demonstrate that meekness correctly understood is a real power in our turbulent world.

Jesus' words well may convey a second meaning. The King's subject who has put "the earth" in proper perspective in his or her system of values really owns it. The individual does not seek it; therefore, it has no hold on that person. The one who seeks the earth can be crushed by it. The one who seeks to further God's kingdom has gained mastery over worldly values. In Eugene Peterson's paraphrase, composed, poised, disciplined Christians "find [themselves] proud owners of everything that can't be bought."

George Buttrick well may have captured the heart of the third Beatitude when he wrote: "The Greek word [for meek] means good will toward man and reverent obedience toward God." Frank Stagg stated: "[The meek] are those who under the pressures of life have learned to bend their wills and to set aside their own notions as they stand before the greatness and grace of God." The meek apply their disciplined strength in serving others in Christ's spirit.

Insatiable Appetite for Righteousness
Matthew 5:6

"Blessed are those who hunger and thirst for righteousness, for they will be filled."

My father was the youngest of ten children. His father died when Dad was 18-months old. Dad often told me of his childhood that was marked by privation. At an early age, he began working to help support the family. The family members literally lived on the edge, eking out a bare living. He told me that many times as a child, he cried himself to sleep because was hungry. Both my parents recounted many scant meals they had during the Great Depression. Sadly, those scenarios were all too common in their childhood and continues in our day in various parts of the world and even in "the land of plenty." Some people live with gnawing hunger and with no assurance of their next meal.

I have never experienced raging hunger that had no prospect of being relieved. The only meals I have missed have been self-imposed in the course of dieting. Even during the lean seminary-student years, the only meal I recall missing I did so when I was so engrossed in working, I neglected to take my lunch break. Of course, I often have reached the point where the low rumbling warnings in my stomach indicated that the body's fuel supply stood on empty. Yet I have never been to the place where I was driven by desperation for want of food. Hunger has never become the constant companion whose gnawing craving becomes an all-consuming drive. I have wanted food, but not in the sense my Dad described or that I see in television reports.

To me, one of the most graphic descriptions of life-threatening hunger is a scene in Jesus' parable in Luke 15:11-32. The prodigal son was in a far country when a severe famine occurred. He became desperately hungry and finally found a job tending pigs. He looked hungrily and longingly at the pods the pigs ate. He felt a strong pull to eat the pods. His raging hunger created a determination to return to his father's house.

A gripping scene of desperate hunger takes place in the movie "Gone with the Wind." Whatever you think of the movie (or the book on which it is based), its depictions of the ravages of the Civil War are gripping. In the scene, the war had come to Tara, the O'Hara plantation. The stately home had been razed and the fields ruined. Scarlet O'Hara went in search of food, and in the area of the slave quarters she found vegetables and began to gather some. Seized with hunger, she unearthed a radish and hastily ate half of it. She immediately upchucked and lay prone. After a while, she uttered a solemn vow: "As God is my witness, as God is my witness, the Yankees aren't going to lick me. I'm going to live through this, and when it's over, I'm never going to be hungry again. No, nor any of my folks. If I have to steal or kill—as God is my witness, I'm never going to be hungry again."

The people of Jesus' day were first-hand acquaintances with hunger. Jesus saw it on every hand as He traveled the roads and paths of his country. Real and prevalent hunger was the reason Jesus' first temptation in the wilderness was so strong and was actually tinged with good. He could exercise His power to turn stones into bread. Not only did He need food after a lengthy period of fasting, but a large number of His people desperately needed food. The average working man in that time earned very little. Compared with what he made, the lowest-paid common laborers today make a fortune. My guess is that obesity was not a problem for most people. Day laborers' families ate meat only once a week, and many people were never far from starvation. The poor subsisted on scant fare. Jesus could use His power to feed the hungry masses, and people would readily follow a Messiah who could provide them with food. In gaining a ready following, Jesus could avoid suffering and death. He rejected the appealing option but retained deep compassion for His people's plight.

I have never experienced ravenous hunger, and neither have I known what desperate thirst is. At various times, I have wanted water badly, and I have been "cotton-mouthed" due to hard, extended labor and participation in athletic contests, I have not experienced the thirst that cracks the lips and saps the strength to the point of immobility. Do not get me wrong—I have been thirsty. I worked for a construction company in the summers between college sessions, and I hand-delivered utility bills year-round during my seminary years. In the intense heat of southern summers, I sometimes had difficulty slaking my thirst. Yet I always knew that good water was not far away.

Most of us have ready access to good, cold, refreshing water. Not so in Jesus' time. Thirst was an ever-present reality for many people. Wells were highly prized, and cisterns for catching and storing water often were matters of life and death. Water was necessary, precious, and sometimes scarce. People understood the meaning of thirst.

Jesus was not the first to use desperate thirst for water to drive home a spiritual truth. In Psalm 42:1-2, the psalmist wrote: "As the deer pants for streams of water, so my soul pants for you, O God. My soul thirsts for God, for the living God." Later in His ministry, Jesus demonstrated His ingenuity by referring to Himself as the bread of life and the water of life. Some of His hearers—those who were receptive—would understand He was asserting He could meet their deepest need; He could give and sustain life on a spiritual level.

In the Sermon on the Mount's fourth Beatitude, Jesus used the physical experiences of hunger and thirst to stress a spiritual principle: Even as hunger and thirst are natural to the human body, so also is a deep drive for righteousness natural to the King's subject. Jesus hardly could have stated this feature of the subject's profile with more force or dramatic impact. He referred to hunger not quickly or partially satisfied and thirst not easily slaked. He had in mind an ongoing, driving, crucial need.

The King's subject is driven by a compelling desire for "righteousness." The term Jesus used means "piety," "godliness," and "fair and equitable dealing." It can have the senses of generosity and alms. It also can convey the ideas of integrity, purity of life, and correctness in thinking, feeling, and acting. To be righteous is to be in a right relationship with God through faith in Christ and to live rightly out of that relationship. Jesus had in mind personal righteousness—personal goodness. The New Testament clearly and emphatically teaches that personal godliness is not an achievement of human effort; it is a constant development that arises out of relationship with God. People related to God through His grace, mercy, and love are in the process of becoming like Him. One of my Old Testament professors in seminary said, in essence: "It is the striking teaching of the Bible that we become like what we worship." To have God at the center of life means to reflect His character, to have a lifestyle that is characterized by integrity, goodness, and exemplary behavior. The King's subjects do this—perhaps slowly, falteringly, imperfectly, and sporadically—but they do it. We work at it because at the center of life, we have been made right. By grace, we have a new standing with God, new life that is sheer gift. We demonstrate this new life in various ways and to various degrees. As the King's willing and obedient subjects, we make progress in demonstrating our personal relationship with Him in the give-and-take of daily life. We strive to have right attitudes and motives and to act rightly. We desperately want to live rightly out of our relationship with Him.

Various translations have attempted to get at the force of Jesus' words. The Holy Bible: Contemporary English Version has: "God blesses those people who want to obey him (or 'who want to do right,' 'who want everyone to be treated right') more than to eat or drink." The New English Bible reads "How blest are those who hunger and thirst to see right prevail (or 'to do what is right')." William Barclay translated "righteousness" as "total righteousness." As these translations show, the term righteousness has several shades of meaning.

Some interpreters have viewed the fourth Beatitude as perhaps the most demanding, for righteousness is a lofty goal. Yet, at the same time, it is one of the most comforting. We can take heart that Jesus did not say, "Blessed are the righteous." Who, having been weighed on God's balances and measured by His tape, could be deemed righteous? None of us could meet

God's high standards. Ours is a history of falling short, of advancing in fits and starts. Yet I firmly believe God gives us credit for our motives and intentions—our determination to "keep at it" in our striving after righteousness.

A good deal of difference exists between lightly saying "I want to be good" and wanting goodness so strongly that we cooperate with God as He produces it. Jesus said the person who longs for righteousness with his/her whole being, for whom it is a constant priority, has God's approval—that individual is on the right track.

The King's subject faces a subtle but powerful temptation: to become content with his or her level or degree of goodness. The person's self-congratulation is all that individual receives. God does not give His stamp of approval. In Matthew 5:20, Jesus warned against self-righteousness. He shockingly declared that unless His hearers' righteousness surpassed the righteousness of "the Pharisees and the teachers of the law," they would "certainly not enter the kingdom of heaven." The Pharisees were Jewish laymen dedicated to keeping all the law—the Ten Commandments and the hundreds of interpretive regulations that were added. Theirs was a works-righteousness, an earned righteousness. The teachers of the law were scribes who began as copyists of the law and then became interpreters and teachers of the law. How could the common people be more righteous than these professionals who were confident they had achieved right standing with God and who displayed impeccable behavior? The implication is that the common people could do so by entering God's kingdom through repenting and placing faith in Christ. They received right standing with God as a gift of grace. They also accepted the demand that they live rightly out that relationship.

The threat to the King's subject is that the person can become content with what William Barclay termed partial righteousness. He made the point that the structure of Jesus' declaration indicates the subject's intense drive is for total, complete goodness. No other goal is higher or more demanding for God's people.

Jesus said that the King's subject who intensely wants righteousness "will be filled." The term Jesus used primarily meant "to feed or fill (animals) with grass or herbage," "to fatten." When it was used to refer to people, it meant "to satisfy with food." It is a strong word that conveys the idea of complete satisfaction. Does this mean the King's subject gains righteousness and wants no more? John A. Broadus, a Baptist scholar of an earlier generation, wrote: "[The word "filled"] does not mean satisfied once for all, so as to have no desire any more (sic)." George A. Buttrick elaborated on this view: "Some hungers, when fulfilled, lead only to satiation....There are other hungers which, once granted, are renewed in higher hunger; and are again fulfilled through further enhancement to eternal life. Such is the hunger for beauty, the hunger for music, the hunger for highest truth." The King's subject finds peace and joy in strengthening his or her relationship with God and in making daily progress in right living.

The intense longing for righteousness has another important aspect. Christians who want to see right prevail rest in God's assurance that His right will prevail. D-Day—Jesus' atoning death and victorious resurrection—has taken place. The victory over evil has been won. Battles go on, but ultimate victory is certain. God's new age, ushered in with Jesus' appearance in human history, moves toward God's goal. People who hunger and thirst for righteousness are those to whom living in the center of God's will is their highest privilege and their first priority. Subjects of the King, they serve Him in loyal obedience. In the process, they grow spiritually.

Merciful

Matthew 5:7

"Blessed are the merciful, for they will be shown mercy."

Mercy begins with God. One of the most important passages in the Bible, both for the ancient Israelites and for us, is Exodus 34:5-7, often called "the proclamation of the name." Verse 6 states: "He [God] passed in front of Moses, proclaiming, 'The Lord, the Lord, the compassionate and gracious God, slow to anger and abounding in love and faithfulness.'" The Hebrew word The Holy Bible: New International Version renders "compassionate" has been translated "merciful," as The King James Version and the Holy Bible: Contemporary English Version have done. A prominent facet of God's character is mercy. In His most complete revelation of Himself in Jesus, God supremely demonstrated His mercy. The strong implication for the King's subject is that the person is to reflect this facet of the King's character.

As the previous Beatitude stressed, the King's subject is to be right, do right, and work to see that right prevails. Yet in the fervent desire to promote right—justice, fairness—kingdom citizens exercise mercy toward people who do not share their purpose and zeal. They also extend mercy toward the needy. The dictionary definitions of the word mercy include: "1. a refraining from harming or punishing offenders, enemies, etc.; kindness in excess of what may be expected. 2. A disposition to forgive or be kind....4. kind or compassionate treatment."

The King's subjects are certain that mercy is one facet of God's character because they have experienced it and continue to experience it. He received us when we had nothing to offer Him; when we repented of our sins and placed our faith in Christ, He forgave us; He continues to deal patiently with us when we disappoint Him; He blesses us when no grounds exist for His doing so. God has made Himself known as our Heavenly Father who expects us to be faithful and to reflect His character in our daily living; yet, at the same time, He is merciful when we fail.

The Scriptures are replete with emphases on God's mercy. Through the centuries the Israelites tenaciously hung on to the truth revealed in Exodus 34:6-7. Deuteronomy 4:31 states: "The Lord your God is a merciful God; he will not abandon or destroy you or forget the covenant with your forefathers, which he confirmed to them by oath." In 2 Chronicles 30:9, the writer noted: "The Lord your God is gracious and compassionate (merciful). He will not turn his face from you if you return to him." Nehemiah 9:17 emphasizes that God is "a forgiving God, gracious and compassionate (merciful), slow to anger and abounding in love," and 9:31 repeats for emphasis that God is "a gracious and merciful God." In Psalm 103:8, the psalmist wrote: "The Lord is compassionate (merciful) and gracious, slow to anger, abounding in love." Psalm 116:5 states: "The Lord is gracious and righteous; our God is full of compassion (mercy)." In Joel 2:13, the prophet wrote that God is "gracious and compassionate (merciful), slow to anger and abounding in love." In his prayer to God, Jonah, the angry prophet, said: "I knew that you are a gracious and compassionate (merciful) God, slow to anger and abounding in love" (Jonah 4:2). The repeated reflections of Exodus 34:6-7 are evidence of the significant place the passage retained in the Israelites' theology (thinking about God). They never forgot that God is merciful, and they counted on His mercy.

The Scriptures admonish God's people to imitate Him. In Ephesians 5:1, the Apostle Paul urged believers to "be imitators of God…as dearly loved children." Albert Barnes asserted: "Nowhere do we imitate God more than in showing mercy." Biblical writers pointed out that God expects His people to be merciful. The writer of Proverbs 11:17, using a different Hebrew word, highlighted the importance of a person's being merciful: "A kind (merciful) man benefits himself, but a cruel man brings trouble on himself." On one occasion, Jesus, the embodiment of God's mercy, said: "Be merciful, just as your Father is merciful" (Luke

6:36). In the fifth Beatitude, He declared: "Blessed are the merciful, for they will be shown mercy." Literally, He said: "Blessed [are] the ones being merciful, for they will be given mercy." The Greek term Jesus used for "mercy" is rich in meaning. It means "pity," "compassion," mercy," and "graciousness." It can have the senses of kindness and good will. In addition, it presents the idea of forgiveness.

To me, mercy is a gold coin with two sides. One side is forgiveness—extending mercy to people who have hurt us. In my experience, forgiving people who have inflicted severe injury on me and my family is one of the most difficult things I am constrained to do as a Christian. I went along for years as a Christian and as a pastor overlooking or tolerating slights I experienced at others' hands, and sadly I preached the need to forgive as though to do so was relatively easy. Then I experienced the deepest and most prolonged pain of my life, and I struggled with extending forgiveness to the person who led in inflicting it. Three insightful fellow Christians helped me come to grips with extending forgiveness.

The first individual was a hospital chaplain who maintained that the first step in forgiving others is to let go of the desire to retaliate or to get even—or more than even. I am convinced that one demonstration of character is what a person does when he or she has the upper hand; when a person has another individual "at his (or her) mercy." The one with the advantage can exact revenge for actual or perceived wrongs, or the person can choose leniency. To exercise mercy is evidence of true strength of character.

The second person to help me was my pastor, who was also a professionally trained counselor. He pointed out that forgiveness is a process. For many people, extending forgiveness comes after a lengthy period of time working through pain and anger to the point of letting the grievance go. I admire and respect people who have suffered tremendous harm at others' hands and who quickly forgive the perpetrators. I do not question their sincerity. Jesus offered the supreme example of forgiveness when He prayed from the cross, "Father, forgive them, for they do not know what they are doing" (Luke 23:34). Later Stephen, the first Christian martyr, prayed as his killers stoned him: "Lord, do not hold this sin against them" (Acts 7:60). Such immediate forgiveness has not been my experience, however. Over time, I came to the point where the memory no longer sparked raw emotion, which I think is another indication of being ready to forgive.

I do not subscribe to the idea that is sometimes put forward that a person has not truly forgiven if the individual has not forgotten the pain inflicted on him or her. I have found that I cannot will myself to forget. To me, memory is mysterious and tricky. It is often triggered by random words, sights, and events. Every now and then, something will bring to mind incidents of my being bullied in high school. I have not been able to erase some memories of hurtful experiences, but I have worked to get rid of anger, bitterness, or resentment.

The third Christian brother who helped me with the matter of forgiveness was a fellow seminary student and much later a coworker at a Christian publishing company. He once told a group of us of an experience of forgiving a person he had held a grudge against for a long period of time. He was present at his daughter's graduation from high school and watched as a young man received his diploma. My friend and coworker had blamed the young man for some of his daughter's problems and bad behavior. The friend said that as he observed the receipt of diplomas, the thought occurred to him that he needed to let his resentment go, to turn it loose, and he did so. Interestingly, one of the Greek terms for forgiveness means "to send away, "to dismiss."

In my mind, an unlikely Old Testament personality offers a classic example of forgiveness as a process. Esau fell victim to his brother Jacob, who conned Esau out of his birthright and accompanying blessing. Esau vowed revenge: When his father died, so would Jacob. Fast forward to a point in time after a span of years. Jacob had fled for his life and now was returning to the promised land. He faced a meeting with Esau, and the outcome was uncertain. When the two came face-to-face, Esau ran to Jacob, embraced him, and both men wept. Jacob said, "To see your face is like seeing the face of God, now that you have received me favorably" (Genesis 33:10). Over the years, Esau had let go of his intense anger and of a desire for revenge.

One side of the gold coin of mercy is extending forgiveness to people who have hurt us deeply. The other side of that coin is compassion and graciousness—good will and kindness extended to the needy. We have a multi-syllable word to describe a merciful, compassionate person: eleemosynary—charitable, giving freely. (I don't use it much because I have trouble pronouncing it.) The King's subject gives freely to people in need, not for show or tax breaks but out of compassion born out of having received the King's compassion. Note carefully that compassion is not merely an emotion. Genuine compassion issues in action; having compassion is being moved so deeply by others' needs that we act to meet the needs. Likewise, kindness and good will take the concrete forms of helpful acts. Truly, mercy is practice. The King's subjects give with no expectation of being "paid back." In fact, they give to people who have no resources to reciprocate.

Jesus said that the merciful are to be congratulated. They have God's approval and His assurance they are on the right path. Jesus stressed they would be "shown mercy." Literally, they would receive (be given) mercy; they would be objects of gracious favor. As they lived in obedient service to God, they would receive mercy. Jesus' assurance could have two shades of meaning. First, believers who extended mercy to others would receive God's mercy. Their openness to give also was an openness to receive. Jesus taught His followers to pray: "Forgive us our debts (offences, sins), as we also have forgiven our debtors" (Matthew 6:12). He added:

"If you forgive men when they sin against you, your heavenly Father will also forgive you. But if you do not forgive men their sins, your Father will not forgive your sins" (Matthew 6:14-15). I don't think He meant God would not be willing to forgive but that He would be unable to do so because the unforgiving person had closed the door on forgiveness.

I once listened intently as a New Testament professor in seminary explained the verses in this manner: When you close a door, it is closed from both sides. Nothing or nobody goes out, and nothing or nobody comes in. When we close the door on forgiving others, we close it on God's forgiveness. We render ourselves incapable of receiving God's mercy. Frank Stagg wrote: "That in one which renders him incapable of being merciful or forgiving also renders him incapable of receiving mercy or forgiveness." Conversely, to forgive is to keep the door open for God's forgiveness to enter the life of the King's subject.

Jesus' words could have a second shade of meaning. Believers who act to meet others' legitimate needs well may find themselves on the receiving end of gifts of mercy when they encounter difficulty. As noted previously, deeds of mercy are not done to gain something in return but acts of kindness often generate reciprocating expressions of care.

In the fifth Beatitude, Jesus emphasized that mercy is active in the life of the King's subject. The Christian extends mercy to others, and both God and others extend mercy to believers. In my prayers, I often ask

God for His mercy and thank Him for making it available. I am reminded repeatedly that receiving mercy carries the demand that I extend it to others.

Pure in Heart
Matthew 5:8

"Blessed are the pure in heart, for they will see God."

The scene must have been electric. In Matthew 23, Jesus addressed the crowds around Him, which included His disciples. The people easily took in His first words, for He instructed them to obey the Pharisees and the teachers of the law. As noted previously (see "Focused on Righteousness"), the Pharisees were a religious sect devoted to keeping all the law—the Ten Commandments and the vast number of rules and regulations that had been added. The teachers of the law were scribes who began as copyists of the law and evolved to be interpreters and teachers of the law. Jesus instructed His hearers to respect these religious leaders' authority. Then, like a sharp clap of thunder, He said: "But do not do what they do, for they do not practice what they preach" (23:3). Their religious practice was for show; it lacked genuineness. Jesus then pronounced seven woes (expressions of grief or denunciation) against the religious leaders, calling them hypocrites—play-actors who hid their true selves behind masks. Jesus' strong words were designed to penetrate the leaders' religious armor and to move them to repentance and faith in Him.

In the course of His stern warning addressed to the religious leaders, Jesus said: "Woe to you, teachers of the law and Pharisees, you hypocrites! You clean the outside of the cup and dish, but inside they are full of greed and self-indulgence. Blind Pharisee! First clean the inside of the cup and dish, and then the outside also will be clean.... You are like whitewashed tombs, which look beautiful on the outside but on the inside are full of dead men's bones and everything unclean. In the same way, on the outside you appear to people as righteous but on the inside, you are full of hypocrisy and wickedness" (23:25-28). Jesus sharply contrasted persona (the image we project) to person (what we really are). He emphasized that we must pay careful, consistent attention to the center of our lives so what we appear to be to others is who we actually are.

In the sixth Beatitude, Jesus congratulated "the pure in heart" (Matthew 5:8). The Greek word for "pure" had a rich background. First, it simply indicated physical cleanliness. Then, it was used to mean "pure," with nothing mixed in. It sometimes referred to freedom from guilt or pollution—moral cleanliness. In a religious context, it was used to indicate someone who was fit to approach God in worship. Finally, it described someone who was genuine, authentic. In the New Testament, the word was used to indicate fitness for God's service and for worshiping Him. It also described a clear conscience.

The word heart was used to refer to the tough little organ that pumps blood through the human body. In the Old and New Testaments, the Hebrew word and the Greek term translated "heart" were used to indicate the center of a person's life, the inner core that was the seat of the emotions, intellect, and will. The heart was where an individual made life-determining decisions; it was the well from which sprang love, hate, anger, and sympathy; it was where thought processes took place; and it was where a person determined courses of action.

The writer of Proverbs 4:23 understood the importance of giving concentrated, continued attention to the inner person: "Above all else, guard your heart, for it is the wellspring of life." Through the prophet Jeremiah, God warned that the inner life can become corrupt: "The heart is deceitful above all things and beyond cure. Who can understand it?" (Jeremiah 17:9). Acutely aware of his sin, David prayed: "Create in me a pure heart, O God" (Psalm 51:10). In Psalm 119:11, the psalmist declared: "I have hidden your word in my heart that I might not sin against you (God)."

The psalmists asked and answered penetrating questions. Psalm 15:1 asks: "Lord, who may dwell in your sanctuary? Who may live in your holy hill?" One of the answers is "he...who speaks the truth from his heart (verse 2). In Psalm 24:3-5, the writer asked: "Who may ascend the hill of the Lord? Who may stand in his holy place?" Then he answered: "He who has clean hands and a pure heart, who does not lift up his soul to an idol or swear by what is false. He will receive blessing from the Lord and vindication from God his Savior."

One of my favorite scriptural prayers is Psalm 19:14: "May the words of my mouth and the meditation of my heart be pleasing in your sight, O Lord, my Rock and my Redeemer." The psalmist sincerely wanted the center of his life to be sound so that what issued from it would meet God's approval.

From childhood Jesus was taught the Hebrew Scriptures and drew from them throughout His public ministry. He would have been thoroughly familiar with the demand that God's people be pure in heart—spiritually sound at the center of their lives. Thus, when he congratulated "the pure in heart," He likely had two prominent ideas in mind: moral cleanliness and singleness of motive.

It is a truism that we live in a day of unrestrained immorality. Moral purity is ridiculed as an archaic idea no longer applicable to a "modern" society. A slogan once trumpeted: "If it feels good, do it." Christians can easily fall victim to a deadly, erroneous concept of salvation and ongoing forgiveness and contribute to what a writer-friend termed the present-day "sexual jungle." One bedrock Baptist doctrine is the security of the believer. A person who makes a genuine faith-commitment to Christ is held securely in His grace.

Regrettably, some come to view this step as a culminating act rather than the beginning of a lifelong spiritual journey of faithfulness, growth, and service. They conclude that because at some point all their previous sins were forgiven and because Christ continues to forgive, they can adopt any lifestyle they choose. This attitude is a deadly misunderstanding of salvation and of continuing grace.

Imprinted indelibly on my memory is an incident that occurred years ago in my long journey as a seminary student. I was eating a meal in the small restaurant directly across the boulevard from the seminary campus. (During those years, I did my part to keep the owner in business.) A man and his young son had finished eating, and the son asked who those people were who went to school across the boulevard. In essence, the father answered: "They are people who believe that when you become a Christian, you can do anything you want to do." Through the years, as the incident has come to mind, I have wondered how the man had formed his opinion. Was he a member of a religious persuasion that had rigid rules and regulations that had to be kept? Had teachers and preachers (or priests) taught him that Baptists generally held that view? Or had he watched the lifestyles of Baptists who were professing Christians and concluded from their conduct that they felt spiritually safe no matter what they did? I am afraid the last possibility well might have been the case.

Christians do not have a rule book to follow as a moral guide, but we have the Bible, especially the life and teachings of Jesus. The greatest incentive for high morals comes from a relationship of shared love with Christ. Authentic believers want to please Him and to represent Him well in a society becoming progressively bankrupt morally. Moral cleanliness is becoming increasingly more challenging because we live in a time when sex before marriage is common and generally accepted. As I was working on this part of my manuscript, I read a newspaper article that stated a noted athlete and his fiancée were expecting their first child, and I was reminded that many in our society actually celebrate impending births outside marriage. In addition, we live in a time when adultery is rampant. Faithfulness in marriage is being taken less and less seriously. Vows repeated in a ceremony can be and too often are easily and casually broken.

My wife and I are members of a coed Sunday School class for senior adults. Among the members are numerous couples who have been married for 50 years and more. They have kept their marriage vows because their exclusive love for each other has allowed no room for third persons to disrupt their relationships. Their determined faithfulness is a badly needed model in a sexually permissive society.

Purity of heart decidedly includes moral cleanliness—adherence to high moral standards. Yet much more is involved. Other religions stress high moral standards; they require correct behavior. Jesus went beneath conduct and stated God's demand for singleness of motive. William Barclay rated the sixth Beatitude as "the most demanding Beatitude of all." As I reflect on

Jesus' words, I am forced to do some soul-searching. It is somewhat painful, but I find this is a place where I must be honest with myself. In his commentary on Matthew, Barclay wrote: "This beatitude demands from us the most exacting self-examination. Is our work done from motives of service or from motives of pay? Is our service given from selfless motives or from motives of self-display? Is the work we do in Church done for Christ or for our own prestige? Is even our Church-going an attempt to meet God or a fulfilling of a habitual and conventional respectability? Is even our prayer and our Bible reading engaged upon with the sincere desire to company with God or because it gives us a pleasant feeling of superiority to feel that we do these things?" These are tough questions that make me uneasy. They force me to be honest with God, myself, and others.

The sixth Beatitude ranks right up there with the fifth in degree of difficulty for me. Too often, as I perform a good deed for someone else, give money for a good cause, or congratulate someone for an accomplishment, I am tempted to pat myself on the back as being seen as a good guy. Sometimes, I become a pleased spectator of my own act. Even acts of ministry can present the temptation to view them as polishing my image. To have unmixed motives is sometimes difficult for me.

Jesus described the person whose purposes are unmixed. Dr. Ray Robbins, one of my New

Testament professors in seminary, stated that God's subject does not try to fool God or other people. Stated another way, the person has no hidden agendas or ulterior motives. The individual could be described as having "an honest heart that aims well." Our word integrity may best pinpoint the force of Jesus' words: "being complete; wholeness, soundness, uprightness, honesty, and sincerity." Purity of heart can be defined succinctly as "a single-minded devotion to God that stems from the internal cleansing created by following Jesus."

I often pray that my persona—the image I project—reflects precisely the person I am. I want my motives, words, and actions to issue from what I am at the center of my being. I continue to work at being a person of integrity. I desperately want to do and say the right things for the right reasons. George A. Buttrick summed up my struggle: "How hard it is to have a 'single eye' [sincerity or purity of mind]! How few…are…without prejudice in their dealings with their neighbors! In politics or trade how few men are thus 'clear' in their intention, and in inner desire how few are even reasonably free from duplicity?"

Jesus declared that people pure in heart "will see God." Interpreters have taken several approaches to these words. One view is that Jesus meant God's people have direct access to Him. At any time and in any place, they can find Him. Specifically, they can enter His presence in prayer and worship; they can seek Him and find Him.

A second view is that this is a promise to be fulfilled in the future. When genuine believers enter eternity to live in God's immediate presence, they will see God face-to-face. In this life, no one can see God and live (see Exodus 33:20). In eternity, the redeemed will be able to view His majestic splendor.

A third approach is that Jesus' words indicate a present reality. In a real sense, believers see God now, in the course of their daily living. George Buttrick wrote that Jesus well may have meant that God's devout subjects see Him in His activities in the world, in the clarity of His will in their lives, and in the guidance of His presence within them. I believe this view captures Jesus' intention. A. M. Hunter wrote that "it is not a matter of optics but of spiritual fellowship."

William Barclay wrote: "It is one of the simple facts of life that we see only what we are able to see; and that is true not only in the physical sense; it is also true in every other possible sense." I do not have to look far to affirm that truth. As a student, I never took an art-appreciation course. I admire paintings because of the scenes, the vividness of colors, and the symmetry, but I cannot enjoy art as someone who is skilled in appraising it. I know next to nothing about flowers. I can tell the difference between roses and dandelions, but that is about it. I have a friend who grows flowers, knows the names of myriads of them, and posts pictures on Facebook with identifying comments. I can look at a structure and admire its shape and materials. My father could look at the same building and see a great deal more because he spent many years helping construct buildings. Indeed, I see what I am able to see. On the spiritual level, I can see God only if I am spiritually conditioned to do so.

Subjects of the King who discipline themselves to retain moral purity and who strive to have unmixed motives see God at work in His world, in other people, and in themselves. Purity of heart is exceedingly difficult to achieve, but it is infinitely rewarding and well worth our continuing efforts.

Peacemakers

Matthew 5: 9

> *"Blessed are the peacemakers, for they will be called sons of God."*

Peacemaking can be, and often is, a risky and sometimes rather dangerous business. I learned this life-lesson the hard way. In one of my pastorates, I was made aware of rather serious conflict between a church staff member and a lay leader. I asked to meet with them to resolve the situation. I was well aware that sometimes, attempting to be a mediator between two parties in conflict may well culminate in both parties' directing their anger at the mediator. That did not happen in my case. What did happen was that when the lay leader realized I would not take sides with her, she began a long and almost successful campaign to have me terminated.

I believe a vital facet of peace-making is having wisdom and insight enough to know when not to step into the middle of a dispute. In my last pastorate, a prominent lay leader approached me with a request that I help him settle a property dispute with a neighbor, who also was a member of the church. I viewed this as a lose-lose situation. If I intervened on his behalf, I would anger and alienate the other person. If I intervened and was unsuccessful, I would invite the anger of the man who asked me to interject myself into the dispute. I declined to get involved, which also probably caused me to lose points with the lay leader, but at least I did not become an unwitting victim of an attempt to manipulate me.

The other side of the coin of peacemaking is that sometimes an attempt's outcome is positive. A friend was concerned that his long-time friendship with one of my church members was cooling. The church member seemed to be distancing himself. Would I encourage the man to communicate with my friend? I was happy to do so, and the relationship strengthened. Peacemaking can be costly, but it also can be rewarding.

Jesus congratulated believers who work for peace, for God approves of people who are willing to run the risk. If we place Jesus' words in the context of His time, we can get some idea of how shocking they were to His listeners. The Holy Land was occupied territory. The hated Romans controlled the Jews' lives, and even though the Romans allowed some measure of freedom, the Jews answered to their occupiers and paid taxes to them. A sect among the Jews advocated violent overthrow of the Romans, and some of them, called the Sicarii ("dagger men"), stealthily assassinated their enemies, mostly Roman officials. Behind this fervent push for freedom stood the rich heritage of the

Maccabees, who had gained a period of freedom for the Jews about two centuries earlier. So evident was the current of insurrection that Jesus warned against the inevitable disaster such a course would bring. The Jews were no match for Rome's might. Their best course was cooperation with the Romans.

One factor that would make for peace would be the Jews' demonstration of good will toward their occupiers. In Matthew 5:41, Jesus said: "If someone forces you to go one mile, go with him two miles." Roman soldiers could compel Jews to carry the soldiers' gear a mile. Going the second mile would be a demonstration of good will that well might have a positive impact on the Romans. On a far more somber note, Jesus warned against the coming destruction of the Jerusalem temple as a result of the Jews' revolt. In this context, Jesus declared that God's genuine subjects worked for peace.

Making peace does involve attempting to resolve conflict, but it includes much more. The Greek word Jesus used for "peace" had a Hebrew background. The Hebrew term shalom (shah lohm) was used as a greeting. It did not convey a negative wish for an absence of conflict. Rather, it was a positive prayer-wish that a person experience good. It conveyed the idea of completeness, wholeness, or soundness. In addition, it could have the senses of health and prosperity, tranquility and contentment. It conveyed the idea of all that made for a person's highest good under God's rule.

Jesus emphasized that the King's subjects seek to resolve conflict and work for others' highest good. A tall order indeed! We have no power to help end hostility on the global stage. We have no cabinet post, no military command. Even in local communities, most of us have little influence. We can only cast our votes for leaders who will work for peace. That is a small contribution, but it is significant. So how can we be peacemakers in situations of conflict?

We can begin with a proper understanding of the peace that comes when we make faith-commitments to Christ and become God's willing, faithful subjects. We are at peace with Him. One of my New Testament professors in seminary described the experience in terms of our laying down our weapons, ceasing rebellion against the King, and surrendering the fortresses of our lives to One who has desired peace all along. This is one way to describe salvation or redemption: Rebels against God make Him Ruler and become His obedient subjects. People who had made God their enemy join His redemptive movement. Life's ultimate issue has been decided, and the result is peace with God.

Peace with God issues in inner peace for God's subjects. Inner peace is not the absence of conflict. As long as we live, we will experience pulls to evil that conflict with God's standards and guidelines. Yet we can live in the confidence that He has made us sound at the center and gives us His presence to help us stay His course. We will not be sin-free, but in His infinite patience God will continue to help us up when we fall;

He will pick us up and put us back in the long-distance race that is the Christian life.

I am convinced we share Paul's experience. In Romans 7:18-19, he wrote: "I have the desire to do what is good, but I cannot carry it out. For what I do is not the good I want to do; no, the evil I do not want to do—this I keep on doing." I believe he was referring to his ongoing battle with evil in his Christian life. In verse 25, he gave ringing thanks to God for triumph through "Jesus Christ our Lord." Paul experienced conflict, but he also experienced victory.

Peace—spiritual peace at the center of life—enables us to be at peace with ourselves. If such a thing as "confessional writing" exists, I engage in it here. One of my lifelong struggles has been to be less critical of myself. In a sermon, my current pastor listed regrets that people had as they approached death. One of these hit home to me. One person said, in essence, that he would not have been so hard on himself; he would have given himself some slack. Part of being at peace with oneself is facing honestly one's positives and negatives and, with God's help, working on the negatives without demanding perfection of oneself and with the understanding that God accepts us, warts and all.

Make no mistake: Peacemaking involves efforts to reconcile people in contention. Yet I also am convinced that Jesus intended for His term "peacemakers" to include persuading people outside the kingdom by choice to become the King's subjects.

Clarence Jordan wrote: "God's plan of making peace is not merely to bring about an outward settlement between evil men but to create men of goodwill." George Buttrick put this truth in different words: "[The peacemaker's] fundamental work is always to reconcile men with God. For as long as men are at odds with God, they are at odds with themselves and with their neighbors." One whom God has made whole wants others to receive soundness or health at the center of their lives. How the King's subjects do this will vary; no one set method is needed. My approach is being ready to tell my story of becoming the King's subject through faith in Christ. In whatever way we do it, our task as peacemakers includes helping bring others into the kingdom.

Jesus said that the peacemakers "will be called sons of God." His words call to mind the familiar phrase "like father, like son." William Barclay noted the phrase stressed that peacemakers would be "doing a God-like work." Two truths are expressed: When we make faith commitments to Christ, we become the King's subjects and are children in His family. The phrase "will be called" likely points to God's recognition of their likeness to Him and to others' recognition of believers' relationship with God. However imperfectly, God's children reflect His character as He has made Himself known. As is true of much in the Christian life, this is a discipline and a process. To experience His grace is to strive to be more gracious; to receive His mercy is to increasingly extend mercy; to know we are loved is to become more loving. The King's subjects become living, daily testimonies to the King's power to transform lives submitted to Him. What greater reward could we want than to be recognized as being like the Ruler and Redeemer of our lives?

Persecuted

Matthew 5:10

> *"Blessed are those who are persecuted because of righteousness, for theirs is the kingdom of heaven."*

Earlier, in comments on the second Beatitude concerning the King's subjects who are grief-stricken over some people's inhumanity toward others, I mentioned my grief and anger concerning the carnage inflicted on people in Syria who are innocent, helpless victims of heartless cruelty and on the volunteer doctors who treat them. I referred to the added dimension such evil has given to my prayers. A second experience has added another dimension. Two African men visited my Sunday School class session. One of them, a former member of my church, told us of their work in their country. He emphasized the intense persecution of Christians, some of whom were killed because of their faith. His riveting words brought home forcefully to me the tragic truth that Christians in some parts of the world suffer greatly for their faith. I remain mindful of these beleaguered saints and pray for them consistently.

The eighth Beatitude presents a difficulty for me: I am not and never have been persecuted because I am a Christian. I have been lumped together with other pastors and opposed with critical sneers by liquor-by-the-drink advocates, but nobody has threatened me. To my knowledge, I am not facing severe opposition at this moment. On the one hand, I am grateful. On the other hand, that circumstance is a source of some concern for me. I have asked myself whether the Christian life can be such smooth sailing as mine seems to be. In order to be opposed, I must stand for something. I must have deep biblical convictions, some of which run counter to my society's currents. I must express my views, some of which will be unpopular. I must be a living contradiction to my culture's progressive permissiveness. Yet, to date I have faced no opposition because of my beliefs.

I have known others who have suffered strong opposition because of their courageous stands as Christians. One man lost his position because of a positive and essentially correct stand on a matter of principle. He and his family eked out a bare living for quite some time. They survived, and he went on to better things. He knew the meaning of persecution. Two seminary students in New Orleans lost their jobs because they made decisions that were different from most residents of the city. They knew what opposition means. A Methodist minister was actively opposed because of his views; his church was damaged, and he was threatened. He knew what being attacked because of his beliefs means.

I have wondered what would happen if Christians seriously and consistently expressed the new life we have in Christ in the current culture. Jesus once said something curious to a man who volunteered to follow Him: "Foxes have holes and birds of the air have nests, but the Son of Man has no place to lay his head" (Luke 9:58). He did not mean He had no homes open to Him. He stayed in the home of Mary, Martha, and Lazarus, and he visited Peter's home. In His response, He meant much more than His lack of a dwelling place. He meant He was not at home in this kind of world. His ideals were different; His standards and principles were different; His view of and approach to life and people were different. The problem of many believers may be that we are far too much at home in our world. We have made our peace with it; we too often conform our lives to its patterns; and we too easily condone mind-sets, lifestyles, and actions that are contrary to the revelation we have in Christ.

The majority of us are not being persecuted—not in the sense of being strongly opposed by people who place entertainment above decency, self-satisfaction above high standards of morality and ethics, selfishness and greed above self-giving love, and desired ends above right means. This truth forces me to pause for reflection. Why do I not meet some measure of resistance from people who do not share my Christian perspective and values?

Consciously or unconsciously, I feel, many of us have become proponents of an inoffensive Christianity. We do not want to offend others by presenting our views too strongly; we do not want to spark others' anger or alienate them. Yet in a real sense, Christianity should offend; our lives should be a strong and clear rebuke to people who are blatant in their wrong; to a society rapidly losing sight of strong, basic moral values; to an evil stance that will not allow others basic rights and opportunities. When Christianity was the world's conscience, it was opposed violently because the way to get rid of a conscience is to kill it. In our culture, the method seems to be to laugh at it as a bothersome relic of a distant and naïve time in the past. You and I have the task of having a lifestyle that contradicts what I consider the blatant paganism of our day.

Jesus said to His hearers, "Blessed are those who are persecuted because of righteousness." Alfred Plummer included a helpful note in his commentary on Matthew: "This last Beatitude does not mean that the ideal Christian character cannot be attained without persecution....It means that, where the Christian character provokes persecution...the Christian has an additional opportunity of proving his sonship and his fitness for the Kingdom." When the quality of the lives of the King's subjects draws unjust opposition, they have the King's approval. They are the kind of people He designed them to be. The Greek word translated "persecuted" basically means "to put in rapid motion" and then "to pursue" with malignant intent. It has the idea of causing someone to flee, to harass the person.

The phrase "because of righteousness" is crucial to an understanding of Jesus' meaning in the eighth Beatitude. Righteousness is right living that issues from a right relationship with God—living by His principles and guidelines revealed in Jesus' life and teachings. Jesus stressed that lives reflecting His character would draw opposition from people who did not share believers' faith-commitments to Him.

We must be clear concerning an important truth. Jesus did not mean we are to set ourselves up as martyrs—to invite others' opposition out of a desire for attention, recognition, or sympathy. Jesus' words allow no room for putting righteous suffering on display.

In addition, Jesus definitely did not mean His followers are to parade their religious piety obnoxiously so that people are not only "turned off" but also react negatively and even forcefully. Judgmental, intolerant, and spiritually arrogant attitudes invite negative responses. Such attitudes can invite opposition we have earned.

Jesus did not congratulate people who cultivated a persecution complex—people who mistakenly felt that others treated them unfairly. He placed no premium on time spent in self-pity. We can waste a lot of valuable time feeling sorry for ourselves because others do not understand us and set themselves against us. As Archibald Thomas Robertson wrote long ago: "Posing as persecuted is a favorite stunt." The Gospels do not contain the slightest hint that Jesus for one moment felt sorry for Himself in the face of constant opposition. Hurt feelings inflicted by others' slights does not translate as persecution.

Jesus was pointing out an obvious truth to His followers: The person who takes up his or her cross and follows Him faces the real possibility of being strongly opposed and even of being maltreated. Some who heard Jesus' words, and many who later chose to follow Him, experienced persecution because of their commitment to Him. Some were disowned by their families; some lost jobs; some lost their lives. Stephen became the first Christian martyr (see Acts 7:59-60). The writer of Hebrews referred to believers who were publicly insulted, persecuted, and imprisoned and to those whose property had been confiscated (see Hebrews 10:32-34). Peter addressed believers who were suffering painful trial and were being "insulted because of the name of Christ" (1 Peter 4:12,14). Jesus was consistently upfront and honest with people who made faith-commitments to Him. His way was not easy, and neither would theirs be. The way of the cross is hard and at times dangerous. Yet it is the only way of life at its fullest.

What would you list as forms of persecution Christians face in our culture's current climate? Several forms come to mind: loss of jobs, expulsion from families, loss of friendships, social ostracism, and insults. To me, the most common form of opposition well may be ridicule. Most of us can take a lot of negative reactions to us, but we cannot take being laughed at or being the butt of jokes because we are viewed as being narrow or overly pious. We do not want to be labeled as prudes, spoil sports, wet blankets, or squares. I think Simon Peter is a biblical example of the effect of ridicule. In the garden of Gethsemane, when the arresting mob came to take Jesus prisoner, Peter was ready to fight to defend Jesus. Later, beside a fire in the high priest's courtyard, he was mocked for being Jesus' follower. In the face of ridicule, Peter denied being Jesus' disciple. Before we begin to denounce Peter, we have to ask how we respond to the growing ridicule of us and our values in our time.

Jesus assured persecuted followers that "theirs is the kingdom of heaven." These words echo those of the first Beatitude. Believers who draw others' opposition because of right relationship with God and the resultant right living are the King's true subjects.

In Matthew 5:11-12, Jesus elaborated on the eighth Beatitude. Believers who were insulted, persecuted, and falsely maligned because they faithfully followed Jesus had God's approval. Persecuted believers could rejoice and celebrate, for they were on the right path, a course of life that culminated in great reward in heaven. The joy to which Jesus referred is not an emotion; it is the confidence of being held in Christ's grace while facing persecution. The word "falsely" stresses opposition that has not been justly earned but issues from evil intent. The persecuted believers stood in the line of God's prophets who preceded them. I believe the reward to which Jesus referred is believers' continued life in God's presence for eternity, what George Buttrick termed "an eternal at-homeness with God." The New Testament contains repeated references to reward for believers. Reward is not the objective toward which Christians strive; reward is the inevitable outcome of faithfulness to Christ. As Archibald M. Hunter phrased it, "The rewards offered by Jesus to the righteous are simply the inevitable issue of goodness in world ruled over by a good God." What reward could be greater than Jesus' commendation: "Well done, good and faithful servant"?

Jesus alerted His followers to expect opposition because their right living contrasted sharply to their pagan culture. Their faithfulness to Him would engender strong resistance. Persecution would be evidence they were on the right path. Today, our task is to make sure that when we are opposed for being Christ's followers, the opposition is not invited or earned.

Believing Without Seeing
John 20:29

> *Then Jesus told him (Thomas), "Because you have seen me, you have believed; blessed are those who have not seen and yet have believed."*

I have selected two additional Beatitudes outside the Sermon on the Mount because they address fairly directly future believers, including today's Christians. Jesus stated one of these shortly before His arrest, crucifixion, burial, and resurrection. He assured future Christians of God's approval. Toward the end of the first century A. D., a heavenly voice directed the aged Apostle John to write a marvelous Beatitude that encouraged Christians undergoing intense persecution. The words contain truth for all believers who maintain their faithfulness under their cultures' pressure to conform.

The first scene was a room in Jerusalem, perhaps the upper room in which Jesus had eaten the Passover meal with His disciples and had instituted His meal His followers were to observe regularly. About a week after

His resurrection, Jesus appeared to 10 of His disciples gathered behind locked doors in the room because they feared the Jews' religious leaders would hunt them down and arrest them. Jesus commissioned them to continue His work and gave them the Holy Spirit (John 20:19-23). Thomas had not been there. When the others told him they had seen Jesus, Thomas declared he would have to see for himself. A week later, Jesus appeared to the disciples in the same room. This time, Thomas was present. When he saw the marks in Jesus' wrists and side, Thomas declared, "My Lord and my God" (20:24-28). Thomas saw the evidence and believed that Jesus had conquered death.

In response to Thomas's declaration of faith and affirmation, Jesus said that Thomas's seeing Him had convinced him that the resurrection was real, and that Jesus lived triumphantly. Then Jesus declared: "Blessed are those who have not seen me and yet have believed" (20:29). The word Jesus used for "blessed" is the same term He used in Matthew 5:3-12. It carries the sense of God's congratulations, His approval. These believers were on the right path in life as Jesus' followers.

The phrase "those who have not seen and yet have believed" may have referred first to believers in the time Jesus spoke who did not have physical evidence of Jesus' being raised to life and thus able to give eternal life—life of distinctive quality that extends into eternity. Yet by extension, Jesus' declaration surely applies to all people through the ages who have made faith-commitments to Him without the benefit of first-hand physical proof. The term "believed" has the ideas of being persuaded of truth and of trusting. Furthermore, it has the sense of obedience and commitment. To believe is to stake one's life on the truth that Jesus is God's Son who is able to give and sustain new life. On the basis of the Scriptures' written witness and of personal experience with the resurrected Christ, countless people have made Jesus Savior and Lord by their faith-commitments. They all have received God's congratulations and approval as people under His gracious rule.

Receiving Consummate Congratulations

Revelation 14:13

> *I heard a voice from heaven say, "Write: Blessed are the dead who die in the Lord from now on." "Yes," says the Spirit, "they will rest from their labor, for their deeds will follow them."*

The time was near the end of the first century A. D. John, the aged apostle, was exiled on the Isle of Patmos because of his allegiance to Christ. Christians were suffering severe persecution, and many were being killed. John received visions that he wrote in order to encourage beleaguered believers to remain faithful to Christ. In one of his visions, he "heard a voice from heaven" (Revelation 14:13). Whether the voice was God's, Christ's, or the Holy Spirit's, the source was Deity. The voice commanded John to write what he heard.

The voice pronounced approval of Christians who died "in the Lord"—people who had made faith-commitments to Christ. These had remained faithful to their Lord, and their faithfulness had led to their deaths. The word the voice used for "blessed" is the same term that occurs in the other Beatitudes. Christian martyrs received God's congratulations for staying the course in their service for Him. The phrase "from now on" points to all future believers who would die because of their faithfulness to Christ.

The Spirit affirmed the blessedness of Christian martyrs. They would "rest from their labor." The Greek word for "rest" also has the idea of being soothed or refreshed. The term for "labor" basically means "to strike" and conveys the sense of beating one's chest in grief. It came to mean sorrow itself. Faithful believers would experience relief from toil that involved emotional as well as physical pain. "Rest" should not be interpreted as idleness. Heaven will not be inactivity. I am convinced that in God's immediate presence, believers will continue to grow, develop, and serve.

The Spirit declared that the faithful Christian martyrs' "deeds [would] follow them." The Greek word for "deeds" differs from the word translated "labors." Believers would be free from painful toil, but their works (actions) would accompany them, "not as merit, nor as personal satisfaction, but in a more solid fashion; for they are to win an innumerable host of converts." An alternate interpretation is that "their endurance, obedience, and faith come along as evidence on their behalf.'

The heavenly Beatitude offered comfort and encouragement to Christians who were facing severe trials because of their faith, but how do the words apply to us? Few of us will be martyred for our faith. I think the following are truths we can glean from the final Beatitude. First, in the face of whatever kind or degree of opposition we encounter because we are Christians, we are to maintain our commitment to Christ. Second, in God's time, we will receive refreshing and ease from any suffering and sorrow we experience because we serve Him. Third, we are assured our efforts of service to God will not be lost but will extend into eternity. As Ray Summers wrote so well: "[The Christian] makes an abundant entrance [into heaven] with all his genuine works for the Lord. He does not go empty-handed as a one-talent servant but as one who has used every opportunity to invest himself profitably for the Lord." Indeed, that is the lofty goal toward which every subject of the King moves.

Today, believers can continue to take courage from the Apostle Paul's exhortation to Christians in Corinth: "Therefore [because ultimate victory is assured in Christ], my dear brothers, stand firm. Let nothing move you. Always give yourselves fully to the work of the Lord, because you know that your labor in the Lord is not in vain" (1 Corinthians 15:58). The work of the King's subject on His behalf will not come up empty but will be productive.

Conclusion

The thesis of this book is that in the Beatitudes Jesus presented a profile of an ideal Christian. He outlined the intended character of the King's subject. I believe any Christian who reads the Beatitudes carefully and prayerfully and studies them seriously will be greatly encouraged but also will be forced to deal with some degree of dismay. Who can measure up to the lofty challenges Jesus' words present? As I worked on my manuscript, I scanned my memory in search of Christians I have known who met all the demands the Beatitudes present, and I came up empty. Some outstanding believers came (or come) close, but no one qualified. Certainly not me. How do we move from realizing we fall short to continuing our efforts to meet the ideal?

For me, determination and incentive arise from my conviction that the King does not give up on His subjects. He continues to work with us to move us toward spiritual maturity. We are imperfect, and we will remain so in this life. Yet we will live in the creative tension presented in Jesus' demand, "Be perfect…as your Heavenly Father is perfect" (Matthew 5:48). Who can do it? No one. Yet no lesser demand would be fitting for God's people. Thus, the ideal is always out there, drawing us toward God's lofty goal for us. I am encouraged by the knowledge that He is with us on the journey, and He is for us. We are His subjects, and we are dearly loved subjects.

Selected Bibliography

Allen, Charles L., *God's Psychiatry* (Westwood New Jersey: Fleming H. Revell Company, 1953)

Arndt, William F. and F. Wilber Gingrich, *A Greek-English Lexicon of the New Testament and Other Early Christian Literature* (Chicago: The University of Chicago Press, 1957)

Ashcraft, Morris, "Revelation" in *The Broadman Bible Commentary,* vol. 12 (Nashville: Broadman Press, 1972)

Barclay, William, *A New Testament Wordbook* (New York: Harper & Row, Publishers, nd)
_____, *The Beatitudes & The Lord's Prayer for Everyman* (New York, N. Y: Harper & Row, Publishers, 1964)
_____, "The Gospel of Luke" in *The Daily Study Bible* (Philadelphia: The Westminster Press, 1956)
_____, "The Gospel of Matthew" in *The Daily Study Bible* (Philadelphia: The Westminster Press, 1958)

Barnes, Albert, "The Gospel According to Matthew" in *Barnes' Notes on the New Testament* (Grand Rapids, Michigan: Baker Book house, 1964)

Blomberg, Craig L., "Matthew" in *The New American Commentary,* vol. 33 (Nashville, Tennessee: Broadman Press, 1992)

Broadus, John A., *Commentary on the Gospel of Matthew* (Valley Forge, Pa.: The American Baptist Publication Society, 1886)

Brown, Francis, S. R. Driver, and Charles A. Briggs, *A Hebrew and English Lexicon of the Old Testament* (Oxford: Clarendon Press, nd)

Bruce, Alexander Balmain, "The Synoptic Gospels" in *The Expositor's Greek Testament,* vol. 1 (Grand Rapids, Michigan: Wm. B. Eerdmans Publishing Company, nd)

Buttrick, George A., "The Gospel According to St. Matthew" in *The Interpreter's Bible,* vol. 7 (Nashville, Tennessee: The Parthenon Press, 1951)

Caird, C. B. "The Revelation of St. John the Divine" in *Harper's New Testament Commentaries* (New York: Harper & Row, Publishers, 1966)

Henry, Matthew, "Matthew to John" in *Matthew Henry's Commentary on the Whole Bible*, vol. 5 (London: Fleming H. Revell Company, nd)

Holman Illustrated Bible Dictionary (Nashville, Tennessee: Holman Bible Publishers, 2003)

Holy Bible: Contemporary English Version (New York: The American Bible Society, 1995)

Hunter, Archibald M., *A Pattern for Life: An Exposition of the Sermon on the Mount* (Philadelphia: The Westminster Press, 1953)

Jordan, Clarence, *Sermon on the Mount* (Valley Forge: Hudson Press, 1952)

Mitchell, Margaret, *Gone with the Wind* (The McMillan Company, 1936)

Owens, John Joseph, *Analytical Key to the Old Testament: Exodus* (San Francisco: Harper & Row, Publishers, 1977)

Peterson, Eugene H., *The Message: The Bible in Contemporary Language* (Colorado Springs, Colorado: NavPress, 2002)
,
Phillips, J. B., "The Gospel of Matthew" in *The Gospels Translated into Modern English* (New York: The Macmillan Company, 1954)

Plummer, Alfred, *An Exegetical Commentary on the Gospel According to S. Matthew* (London: Elliot Stock, 1910)

Robertson, Archibald Thomas, "The Gospel According to Matthew" in *Word Pictures in the New Testament,* vol. 1 (Nashville, Tennessee: Broadman Press, 1930)

Roget's International Thesaurus (Thomas Y. Crowell Company, 1962)

Severance, W. Murry, *Pronouncing Bible Names* (Nashville, Tennessee: Broadman & Holman Publishers, 1994)

Stagg, Frank, "Matthew" in *The Broadman Bible Commentary,* vol. 8 (Nashville, Tennessee: Broadman Press, 1969)

Summers, Ray, *Worthy Is the Lamb* (Nashville, Tennessee: Broadman Press, 1951)

Thayer, Joseph Henry, *Greek-English Lexicon of the New Testament* (Grand Rapids, Michigan: Zondervan Publishing House, 1970)

The Analytical Greek Lexicon (New York: Harper & Row Publishers, nd)

The Cambridge Advanced Learner's Dictionary & Thesaurus c Cambridge University Press

The Holy Bible: King James Version (Grand Rapids, Michigan: Zondervan Bible Publishers, nd)
The New English Bible (Oxford University Press, Cambridge University Press, 1970)

Vincent, Marvin R., "The Gospel According to Matthew" in *Word Studies in the New Testament,* vol. 1 (Grand Rapids, Michigan: Wm. B. Eerdmans Publishing Co., 1965)
_____, "The Revelation of John" in *Word Studies in the New Testament,* vol. 2 (Grand Rapids, Michigan: Wm. B. Eerdmans Publishing Co., 1965)

Webster's New World Dictionary of the American Language (Nashville, Tennessee: The Southwestern Company, 1969)

Williams, Charles B., *The New Testament in the Language of the People* (Nashville: Holman Bible Publishers, 1986)

www.ingramcontent.com/pod-product-compliance
Lightning Source LLC
Chambersburg PA
CBHW052202110526
44591CB00012B/2043